Handbook on Patents for Scottish Solicitors

J. & J. Jack,

W.S.

HANDBOOK ON
PATENTS

FOR SCOTTISH SOLICITORS

By R. M NEILSON

Whitworth Exhibitioner
Member of the Institution of Mechanical Engineers
Member of the Institution of Engineers and Shipbuilders in Scotland
Member of the West of Scotland Iron and Steel Institute

CHARTERED PATENT AGENT

Author of

The Steam Turbine '
" Aeroplane Patents '
' The Protection of Trade Designs '

GLASGOW
Printed by Fraser, Asher & Co , Ltd , 73 Dunlop Street
1914

PREFACE.

Scottish solicitors are often consulted on matters relating to patents; and the present handbook has been prepared with the object of affording them a ready means of reference with regard to many questions which may arise.

There are several good books on patent law, and this little volume cannot, and makes no attempt to, displace them. These larger books do not, however, give the solicitor all the information and advice that he may desire, and, moreover, the (commendable) attempt of their authors to state the law in its entirety, and elucidate it with adequate examples and references to Law Court decisions, often demands from the consulter the perusal of a large amount of matter in order to get the desired information.

In the present book the several matters dealt with have been treated as concisely as possible, but in the case of such subjects as assignations and licences it has been necessary to speak somewhat lengthily in order that the necessary information and advice might be given.

The author will be glad to receive suggestions in regard to additional matter which, in the opinion of readers, might advantageously be included in a future edition.

R. M. N.

Atlantic Chambers,
45 Hope Street, Glasgow.
August, 1914.

CONTENTS

HANDBOOK ON PATENTS

FOR SCOTTISH SOLICITORS.

What Can be Patented.

A valid British patent can be obtained only for what is new, is useful, and involves invention. Novelty alone is not sufficient, nor yet novelty combined with usefulness. The discovery of a new physical law cannot be patented even although the discovery may be, not only of academic interest, but also of practical value. The invention, however, of apparatus to take advantage of a new discovery may be good subject-matter for a patent. Moreover, novelty and invention are not sufficient without usefulness; and a patent may be upset for absence of utility. A patent for a useless invention may be a hindrance to industry, and can only be of profit to the patentee through intentional or unintentional deception.

Novelty, according to British law, means novelty within the United Kingdom. Prior knowledge of the invention abroad, even in a British Colony, is no bar to the obtaining of a valid British patent, so that an invention which has been publicly exhibited abroad, but not described in any printed publication in circulation, or in any manuscript or book or pamphlet accessible in a public library, within the United Kingdom, may still be patented in Great Britain.

Moreover, an inventor is not debarred from obtaining a valid patent for an invention by reason of this having previously been invented by another party and tried in secret within the United Kingdom. It frequently happens that two persons independently invent substantially the same thing Priority is then accorded to the first of the two who applies for the patent, even although the other party was the first to invent.*

There is an exception to the requirements as to absence of prior publication in the United Kingdom, which is, that an invention forming the subject-matter of a British patent applied for on or after January 1st, 1905, is not held to be anticipated by reason only of its publication in the specification of a British patent applied for fifty years or more before the date of application for the patent in question, or its publication in a British provisional specification of any date not followed by a complete specification (The present practice of withholding publication of provisional specifications not followed by complete specifications was not always in vogue.)

---

* See, however, remarks on "International Convention" on page 36.

A further exception to anticipation by prior publication is made in the case of publication of an invention at, or in connection with, an industrial or international exhibition certified as such by the Board of Trade, provided that the applicant gives notice, if required, of his intention to exhibit, and applies for a patent not later than six months after the date of opening of the exhibition

What Constitutes "Invention."

It has been said that invention is essential in order to obtain a valid patent.   Whether a certain change in design does or does not comprise invention has been the subject of many a lawsuit, and the subject is treated very fully in several of the larger works on Patents. No attempt will be made to discuss the subject here, except to give the following advice which experience has shown to be generally good   The inventor or designer should put to himself the question : Is the improvement so natural and so obvious that an intelligent workman engaged in the manufacture of articles of the nature of that on which the improvement has been effected, and having a knowledge of all that has already been done of a relevant nature, would in nine cases out of ten think of the improvement in question?   If the answer to the query is in the affirmative there is probably not sufficient invention to support a patent, if in the negative there probably is.

The magnitude of the divergence from known practice is no criterion of the existence or absence of patentable invention; and a mere rearrangement of parts or simplification of a process or construction may afford good subject-matter for a patent. In many cases the inventor or improver will not be able to decide with confidence whether or not he has good subject-matter for a patent, and the point can only be decided by one who has expert knowledge of patents.

Patents and Designs.

Certain novel and useful improvements can be protected by registering the design. It is cheaper to register a design than to obtain protection by means of a patent; and the question often arises as to which means, or whether both means, should be chosen to obtain protection. In debating this question it is important to note that, in considering whether a new design is sufficiently novel and distinctive to be registrable, and also in considering whether a registered design is infringed by one somewhat similar, the reason for adopting the design, and the utility of the design, must be put in the background and the eye alone employed to detect novelty, originality, or distinctiveness.

It will be obvious that this reliance on the eye has often an important bearing on the protection afforded by registration. For example, an engineer might conceive a new design for a part of a machine which possessed decided advantages but which might be of such a nature that it could be imitated, and the same effect obtained, by many other designs which, judged by the eye alone, were all considerably different from the original. Registration of design would in such a case afford little protection; but, if the purpose of the innovation were new, a patent could be obtained. It sometimes happens, however, that, even as regards a part of a machine which is not exposed to public view, and in which appearance is no consideration, the virtue of a particular configuration lies in the precise design adopted : in such a case registration of design affords all the protection possible and is easier and cheaper to obtain, and is more quickly procured, than a patent. A design for registration does not require to be ornamental.

The term of a patent is fourteen years, which only in particularly exceptional circumstances can be extended.* A design is registered in the first instance for five years, an extension period of another five years being afterwards securable; and, with the consent of the Comptroller-General of Patents, a second extension period of five years may be obtained. The full term of registration for a design may thus be fifteen years.

---

* See page 34

Who Can Apply for a Patent.

Any individual or individuals, whether resident in the United Kingdom or abroad, and whether a British subject or not, can apply for a British Patent, provided that this individual is, or these individuals are, or include, the inventor or inventors. That is to say, in the case of a single applicant, he (or she) must be the inventor; and, where there are two or more applicants, the inventor, or all the inventors, must be included; but it should be noted that one or more non-inventors may apply jointly with the inventor or inventors. A corporate body may be joint applicant with the inventor or inventors, but cannot of course be sole applicant as it cannot invent. A firm may apply in the names of the several partners alone if these include the inventor or inventors or may apply under its trading name jointly with the inventor or inventors who may or may not be a partner or partners.

An application for a patent for an invention of a deceased inventor may be made by his legal representative who must prove his title.

The above remarks apply to ordinary cases in which the usual application form is used. The case of inventions applied for by a communicatee is dealt with in the paragraph immediately following; and applications for

"Patents of Addition," and "Convention" applications, are dealt with in later paragraphs.*

Communicated Inventions.

An invention may be communicated from abroad (*i.e.* from outside the United Kingdom) to a person resident within the United Kingdom. A patent may then be applied for by the communicatee in his own name, mention being made of the communicator. A special application form is required in this case. The advantage of this procedure—which is quite optional—is that none of the necessary documents require to be filed with the signature of the communicator. All that is demanded of an inventor or of the possessor of an invention abroad is that he send a description of the invention and instructions for an application for a patent to a person resident in the United Kingdom (usually a patent agent) who can then apply for a patent in his own name. The patent when granted can be assigned by the communicatee to the communicator or held in trust for him. The communicator is not necessarily the inventor.

Joint Patentees.

As it is common for two or more persons to combine to apply for a patent, the respective rights of the two

---

parties are of interest.   It should be noted in the first place that, if one of the applicants is the inventor and the other is not, the law makes no distinction between the two : each has the same rights as the other.   Moreover, whether one or more of the patentees are inventors, any one of them has, in the absence of an agreement, the right to work the invention without accounting to his colleague or colleagues; but no one of them can grant a licence without the consent of the other or others, as the case may be.   The law with respect to independent working by either patentee is a strong argument in favour of a working agreement being arranged at an early date, especially in the case of an inventor who is not himself in a position to manufacture and who combines with a manufacturer to obtain and exploit a patent for his invention   In the absence of an agreement to the contrary, the manufacturer can work the invention without the approval of the inventor and without giving any remuneration to the latter.

If, in the case of a patent dated on or after January 1st, 1908, one of the co-patentees dies during the term of the patent, his beneficial interest in the patent devolves on his personal representatives as part of his personal estate. In the case, however, of a patent dated prior to January 1st, 1908, if one of the co-patentees dies, his interest passes to the surviving patentee(s) unless their relations are modified by contract.

As a rule it is better that co-patentees should have an agreement in writing, no matter how intimate and friendly may be their relationship to each other.

Master and Servant.

In the absence of an agreement to the contrary, it is quite competent for an employee to apply for a patent for his own invention, even if the subject-matter of the invention is relevant to the work on which he is employed and for which he is paid. It would be fraud, however, for an employee to apply for a patent for an invention which originated with his employer and which he had simply developed on his employer's instructions. An employer is quite entitled to use his employees to assist him in working out his ideas and in improving them, and he can then, quite rightly, apply for a patent in his own name alone. Moreover, an employer may ask his employees to sign an agreement to the effect that they will not apply for any patents without first obtaining his consent; and, without any specific agreement on the subject, the terms on which an employee is engaged or employed may render a particular invention the property of his employer.

When an employee gives up his rights with regard to *his own* invention to his employer, it is not allowable for the latter to apply for a patent in his own name alone : the inventor must be the applicant or a joint applicant. In all cases where an employer wishes to have the patent rights of inventions of his employee, a written and stamped agreement is to be recommended

Steps to be Taken in Applying for a Patent.

The law gives to the applicant for a patent the choice of applying direct to the Patent Office or applying through an agent whom he authorises; and there is no restriction as to who may act as agent as long as he is resident, or has a place of business, in the British Isles. The preparing of an application for a patent with the accompanying specification of the invention is, however, a matter requiring considerable skill; and the legal mind will readily perceive that the filing of an application without the employment of an agent is not a course to be recommended, and that what is still more to be dis-couraged is the employment as agent of a person who is not fitted to act as such.

The names of all persons entitled to describe them-selves as patent agents are entered on the official register, and a warning may here be given that some unscrupulous persons, who are not on the register, and are not entitled to describe themselves as patent agents, seek to evade the law and obtain patent agency work by calling themselves " Patent Experts," or their places of business " Patent Bureaux," or the like. The Comptroller, except in a few cases, has no power to refuse to receive applications for patents filed through such parties.*

The application for the patent should be made before the public is allowed to see the invention; but the invention may be worked in secret, or shown, or described in confidence, to one or more individuals before the date of application It is desirable to take all reasonable precautions to prevent the invention being known to the public before the date of application; but any disclosure through breach of faith will not be a bar to the grant of a valid patent if the applicant lodges his application without undue delay after hearing of the disclosure of the invention.

Application for a Patent must be made on one or other of five forms (Patents Forms Nos. 1, 1A, 1B, 1C, or 1D)

---

* A copy of the Official Register, containing the names and addresses of all Patent Agents, can be obtained from Messrs Eyre & Spottiswoode, Ltd , East Harding Street, London, E.C. Price 1s; postage 1d. A list containing the names and addresses of all *Chartered* Patent Agents can be obtained gratis from the Secretary of the Chartered Institute of Patent Agents, Staple Inn Buildings, London, W.C.

according to the circumstances.   The form is usually prepared or filled up by the patent agent, but it must be signed by the applicant or applicants (in the case of a communicated invention the patent agent may be the applicant*) who must declare that he or they or one or more of them claims or claim to be the inventor or inventors.   The form should be filled in before signature.   It must bear a £1 stamp and when filed must be accompanied by either a provisional or a complete specification of the invention, and, if an agent is employed, by an authorisation of such agent.   Provisional and complete specifications must be drawn up as prescribed; there is also a prescribed form of authorisation of agent.

A provisional specification is unstamped, but a complete specification must bear a £3 stamp.   An authorisation requires no stamp.   The total stamp fees on application are therefore £1 or £4 according to whether a provisional or a complete specification is filed.

Provisional Protection.

When a provisional specification is filed, the applicant is said to apply for " provisional protection," which lasts for six months or, by paying an extension fee, for seven

---

* See page 13.

months. Before the expiry of this period a complete specification must be filed or the application will lapse. The invention does not require to be described with the same detail in a provisional as in a complete specification, and with the former drawings are not as a rule required. Moreover, in a provisional specification the applicant's claims do not require to be particularly formulated.

In the majority of cases it is the better course to file a provisional specification in the first instance, because the trials of the invention under service conditions may suggest small, but sometimes very important, improvements which in many cases may be incorporated in the complete specification, or the experience or knowledge acquired during the period of provisional protection may suggest to the applicant the framing of his claims in a way which he would not have adopted had he filed a complete specification in the first instance. It is usually unsafe to put the invention into service until a patent has been applied for.

What is often, however, a more important consideration is the fact that the filing of a provisional specification in the first instance puts the applicant to less initial expense; also, before it is necessary to file a complete specification, he may have entered into business relationship with a manufacturer—if not a manufacturer himself.

Moreover, during the interval he may acquire experience or knowledge which shows him that it will be advisable to cut his losses and abandon the application.

Complete Specification After Provisional.

As already mentioned an application for a patent filed with a provisional specification lapses unless followed by a complete specification. The latter must be filed within six months of the filing of the application unless an extension of time, of one month's duration, is applied for (on a prescribed form) and a late fee (£2) paid. No further extension of time is obtainable.

A complete specification following a provisional must bear a £3 stamp, so that the stamp fees ultimately paid are the same whether or not a provisional specification is filed.

A complete specification following a provisional should in general be confined to the same matter as is contained in the provisional, but the description is generally fuller and more detailed. The inclusion of matter not fore-shadowed in the provisional but of use in elucidating the invention will not always be objected to provided that no claims are made for anything not referred to in the provisional If, however, claims are made for what the examiner considers has not been referred to in the provisional specification, these claims will have to be cancelled (They may be included in a separate application for patent.) Alternatively, the provisional specification may be abandoned, and the application for patent considered as if filed with the complete specification. (In this case the original date is of course lost.)

One complete specification can embody the subject-matter of two or more provisional specifications which in the opinion of the examiner are sufficiently allied to each other. In this case one patent only is granted, a saving in fees being thus effected. The complete specification must be filed not later than six months—or, on payment of the prescribed late fee, seven months—after the filing of the first provisional. The second—or, if there are more than two, the last—provisional can, if desired, be filed on the same day as the complete specification.

Complete Specification in First Instance.

In many cases, however, in order to get the full advantage of a patent at as early a date as possible, it is desirable to file a complete specification in the first instance, i e with the application form, no provisional specification being then lodged. The privileges and rights pertaining to the patent are obtained in part when the complete specification is " accepted " * and in part when the patent is thereafter sealed.†

It is sometimes advisable to file a complete specification in the first instance for another reason—to get the result of the official search as soon as possible.‡

Drawings and Samples.

Drawings are required to be filed with a complete specification when necessary to make the invention clear. With the exception of chemical inventions—in the case of which the Patent Office may call for samples or specimens—it may be said that drawings are generally indispensable Drawings may be called for by the Patent Office in the case of provisional specifications, but this proceeding is rare. In some cases it is advisable in the applicant's interest to file drawings with a provisional specification; and, in such a case, if the draw-

---

* Acceptance of complete specification is explained on page 27, under the heading " Opposition to Patent."

† " Sealing of Patent " is explained on page 32.

‡ See sections " Search as to Novelty," page 23, and " Amendment to meet Official Objections," page 24.

ings (without alteration) are suitable for use with, and are sufficient to illustrate the description in, the complete specification, new drawings are not required to be filed with the latter. All drawings must be executed in a prescribed manner and supplied in duplicate.

Search as to Novelty.

The inventor is always more or less in doubt as to the novelty of his invention, and the question often arises as to whether he should institute a search through the patent records with the object of reducing the uncertainty to a minimum. An invention may, of course, be anticipated by some publication not to be found in the patent records; but a thorough search made by a competent person familiar with the official method of abridging the specifications and having the necessary technical knowledge will, as a rule, leave only a small chance that anything which would anticipate the invention exists and has not been found.

When a complete specification is filed either in the first instance or following a provisional specification, the Patent Office makes a search through the British patent records for 50 years back as to the novelty of the invention. It is therefore often good policy for the inventor to save expense by applying for a patent without previously making any search, and this is the course which is usually adopted. When, however, it is proposed to spend much money on the invention before the result of the British Patent Office search is made known, it is generally to be recommended that a patent agent be instructed to make a search. Of course a patent agent may, without making a search, be able to inform the inventor of some prior patent which will affect him, but he cannot be expected to be familiar with all that is contained in the patent records.

A search, if decided on, should be done well. It is often an expensive matter, the expense depending on the nature of the invention.

Amendment to Meet Official Objections.

If the official search discloses any prior patent which is thought to affect the application in question, the applicant is notified of this prior patent and allowed to amend his specification to meet it. If no amendment is made which satisfies the Comptroller, he may make a reference to the prior specification at the end of the applicant's specification or may refuse to grant a patent. An officially-made specific reference to a prior specification is usually considered as damaging.

The applicant, on receiving the examiner's report on the result of the official search, or after correspondence thereon, may abandon the application In that case no Government fees paid are returned to him, but he saves the sealing fee *

Particulars Required by Patent Agent.

In order to obtain the utmost protection possible and obtain the strongest possible patent, it is desirable that the patent agent be supplied with full particulars of the invention It is especially necessary for him to know the characteristic feature or features of the invention— the point or points in which it differs essentially from what has been done before, it is therefore necessary in many cases that he should be informed of other and known constructions or processes which come near to the invention which it is desired to protect. Some inventors are inclined to hold back information which might depreciate their invention Sometimes this is done intentionally, and at other times unconsciously. It is a practice to be avoided In the belief that the applicant is entitled to broader claims than he really is, the patent agent may insert claims which may be objected to by the

---

* For sealing fee see page 32

examiner and so cause unnecessary trouble; or the examiner may pass the claims, and an invalid patent result

Moreover, the withholding of information may mislead the patent agent as to the real gist of the invention and cause the whole specification to be drawn up according to a wrong scheme which cannot be satisfactorily put right by amendment after the specification has once reached the Patent Office.

It cannot be too much emphasised that, in order to obtain the utmost protection for an important invention, it is necessary that the patent agent should combine with a knowledge of patent law and procedure, not only a mind's eye view of the physical aspect of the invention, but a thorough appreciation of the characteristic idea which is its distinguishing feature.

The above remarks apply, not only when a complete specification is to be drafted, but also in the case of a provisional specification. The claims which will be allowed in a complete specification following a provisional depend greatly on the contents, and sometimes on the wording, of the provisional specification.

It is often desirable that the patent agent be supplied with a written description and a drawing or drawings of the invention, and this sometimes holds good even in connection with the preparation of a provisional specification which is to be filed at the Patent Office unaccompanied by drawings. In other cases a verbal description is quite sufficient. If drawings or models have been prepared to assist the inventor or his associates, it will usually be advantageous to submit these to the patent agent; but otherwise it is suggested that the inventor should not be advised to put himself (or others) to much expense in the matter of drawings or models until he has consulted a patent agent.

Opposition to Grant of Patent.

When a complete specification has been passed as in order by the Patent Office examiner, it is " accepted " (unless it is desired to delay acceptance *) and the acceptance is advertised in the Official Journal of Patents. Opposition to the grant of a patent can be lodged any time within two months from the advertisement of acceptance. The specification is open to public inspection at the Patent Office on acceptance, and printed copies of the specification are on view and on sale at the Patent Office about three weeks after acceptance.

---

* Remarks on delaying acceptance are given on page 39.

[Opposition to Grant]

Some firms directly, or through their patent agents, watch for applications for patents which, if granted, would adversely affect them. It involves much less expense to oppose the grant of a patent than afterwards to bring an action to have the patent revoked.

Opposition actions are heard before the Comptroller, and appeal from his decision may be made to the Law Officer (the Attorney-General or Solicitor-General for England) There are four statutory grounds of opposition and none other is competent.

First Ground :

The first ground is that the applicant obtained the invention from the opponent, that is, from the person who is opposing the grant of the patent, or from a person of whom the opponent is the legal representative When this is the ground of opposition, the Comptroller considers statutory declarations and evidence given in court by witnesses; and decides as to whether or not the opponent has made out his case. The Comptroller will not refuse a patent unless he is convinced that the opponent has made out his case If he should be in some doubt on this point, he will grant the patent. The same remarks apply to the Law Officer. This is only fair and reasonable, because, if a patent is unjustly refused, a great injury is inflicted on the applicant, whereas, if the decision goes against the opponent, he can always bring an action at a subsequent date to revoke the patent, or he can infringe the patent and defy the patentee to stop him.

If it is decided by the Comptroller, or by the Law Officer, that both the applicant and the opponent have contributed materially to the invention, the applicant may be granted the patent after portions are struck out which were due to the opponent, or the Law Officer may direct that the patent be granted without amendment of the specification but impose terms which give both parties an interest in the patent.

It has been decided that it is not the duty of the Comptroller or the Law Officer in an opposition action to inquire into whether or not the applicant obtained the invention from the opponent *abroad*, and, in the case of an invention communicated from abroad, it is not their duty to inquire as to who was the actual inventor or as to how the communicator obtained the invention.

Second Ground:

The second ground of opposition is that the invention has been claimed (note *claimed*—not merely described) in a complete specification for a British patent which is or will be of prior date to the patent the grant of which is opposed. The prior specification relied on must, how-

[Opposition to Grant]

ever, be that of a patent applied for not more than fifty years before the date of application for the patent which is being opposed   The specification relied upon need not be that of an actual patent : it may be that appertaining to an application of prior date on which the patent has not yet been granted.   The complete specification must, however, have been accepted.

In order that the opponent may succeed in an opposition action on the second ground, it is necessary for him to convince the Comptroller that, in the prior specification relied on, substantially the same invention is claimed as that in the opposed patent.   If the Comptroller considers that the subject-matter of the claims in the opposed patent has some substantial improvement not claimed in the prior specification, he will not refuse a patent, and, if he is in doubt on the point, he will probably give the applicant the benefit of the doubt, that is, he will grant a patent.

In many opposition actions when the second ground is relied upon, the Comptroller does not absolutely refuse to grant a patent, but makes the grant of a patent conditional on the applicant so amending his specification as to indicate what has previously been done by the opponent, or by another party or parties ; such amendment has to meet with the Comptroller's approval before he will pass the applicant's specification and allow the patent to be sealed In some cases the Comptroller may order that the applicant shall in his specification particularly refer to the patent cited by the opponent. In other cases he may only require a general statement.

Third Ground:

The third ground of opposition is that the nature of the invention or the manner in which it is to be performed is not sufficiently or fairly described and ascertained in the complete specification. Patents are not often opposed on this ground alone.

Fourth Ground:

The fourth ground of opposition is that the applicant's complete specification describes or claims an invention other than that described in his provisional specification and that such invention forms the subject-matter of an application for patent made by the opponent in the interval between the leaving of the applicant's provisional specification and the leaving of the applicant's complete specification. If the application relied on by the opponent is a convention application,* the date of filing in Great Britain must be prior to the date of the applicant's filing his complete specification.

---

* Convention application is discussed on page 36.

[Opposition to Grant]

Opposition on the first or fourth ground is obviously by an interested party. An opponent relying on the second or third ground must show that he is interested. It has been ruled by the Comptroller that the possession in a *bona-fide* and honest manner of an article which may reasonably be held to fall within the scope of the applicant's claims gives an opponent a *locus standi* on the second and third grounds.

If the applicant and the opponent come to terms, a hearing may be avoided; and an amendment of the specification agreed upon by the applicant and the opponent may be accepted by the Comptroller without a hearing. The avoidance of a hearing saves expense, especially if the applicant, or opponent, and patent agent are resident in Scotland.

The applicant, when opposed, may voluntarily abandon his application without a hearing, and, if the sealing fee (see next paragraph) has been paid, he can recover the value of this. He may, however, be required to pay costs to the opponent.

Sealing of Patent.

A patent is usually sealed—*i.e.* the Letters Patent granted and issued to the applicant—about eleven weeks after acceptance of the complete specification, provided that there is no opposition and that the sealing fee has been paid. The sealing fee (£1) can be paid any time after acceptance of the complete specification.* After sealing, the applicant becomes the patentee.

Duration of Patent—Renewal Fees.

The normal term of a British patent is fourteen years, but in order to keep the patent in force for this period it is necessary to pay renewal fees commencing at the end of the fourth year of the term. The renewal fee increases by £1 a year from £5 at the end of the fourth year to £14 at the end of the thirteenth year. The applicant for a patent does not incur liability to pay these fees, but if they are not paid, the patent lapses. The term of the patent is reckoned from the date of application in Great Britain except that, when an earlier date is claimed in virtue of an earlier application in another convention country,† or for other reason, the term is reckoned from this earlier date.

---

* The aggregate government fees which have to be paid before a patent is granted amount to £5—viz , £1 on the application form, £3 on the complete specification, and £1 on applying for sealing.

† The term " Convention country " is explained on page 36.

c

Late Payment of Renewal Fees—Restoring Lapsed Patent.

A renewal fee may be paid late—to the extent of three months—by applying for extension of time and paying the required late fee (£1 to £5); this application for extension of time may be made when the renewal fee is actually paid. It is not necessary to give any reason for the delay of payment of annuities (up to three months): the delay may be either intentional or through neglect or mishap.

After the three months' extension period has expired, the patent becomes void; if, however, the omission to pay the renewal fee is unintentional, and no undue delay occurs in applying for restoration of the patent, the Comptroller *may* restore the patent. Restoration of a lapsed patent is a somewhat expensive matter (although not nearly so costly as formerly, when a special Act of Parliament was necessary), the stamp fee alone on the application being £20.

Extension of Term of Patent.

An extension of the term of a patent beyond fourteen years can sometimes be obtained on petition to the Court, if it can be proved that the patentee has been inadequately remunerated, taking into account the nature and merits of the invention. It is not worth while incurring the expense of an application for extension of term unless a very good case can be put forward; and it may here be mentioned that the Court may be greatly concerned with the remuneration of the original patentee and show little or no concern with the remuneration of any individual or company who may have acquired or be working the patent

Secret Patent.

If an inventor of any improvement in instruments or munitions of war assigns the benefits of his invention to the Admiralty or the War Office before applying for a patent, or before his complete specification is published, an Admiralty or War Office certificate is sent to the Patent Office, and the application for patent then receives special treatment with a view to secrecy. If the assignation is made prior to the filing of the application for patent, a special application form is required, and the certificate aforesaid is filed at the Patent Office at the same time.

Surrender of Patent.

When a patentee wishes his patent to lapse, his usual procedure is purposely to omit to pay the next renewal fee. The patent then automatically becomes void. A patentee may, however, at any time offer to surrender his patent, and in this case he applies to the Comptroller on a prescribed form.   The Comptroller on receiving the application gives notice of the offer and hears any party who desires to be heard and, if he thinks fit, orders the revocation of the patent.   A patentee holding an invalid patent may, in certain cases, be well advised to surrender the patent so as to avoid the risk of having to submit to an order for revocation and pay the costs of the petitioner even when the order is made by consent.

Colonial and Foreign Patents; International Convention.

A British patent gives protection only in Great Britain, Ireland, and the Isle of Man.   An invention can, however, be protected in most of the important British possessions and foreign countries by separate application. It would be impossible in this volume to give even a summary of the laws in the various British possessions and foreign countries; but a few remarks may be made about applying for patents abroad. Great Britain and certain British Colonies, together with a large number of the more important foreign states, are signatories to an International Convention, and, by one of the clauses of the Convention, a British inventor can file applications for patents in the other Convention countries any time within twelve months from the date of his application in Great Britain, and can secure for these applications the benefit of the British date. An inventor has, therefore, ten or eleven months from the date of filing his application in Great Britain in which to ascertain how his invention is likely to turn out in service; in which to obtain, if necessary, financial assistance; and in which to assign his rights, or grant, or arrange to grant, licences.

The Convention countries are as follows :—

Great Britain.
Australia.

Ceylon.
New Zealand.

Trinidad and Tobago

Austria.
Belgium.
Brazil
Cuba.
Denmark with
    Faröe Islands.
France with Colonies
Germany
Hungary.
Italy.
Japan
Mexico.

Netherlands with Dutch
    East Indies, Surinam,
    and Curaçoa.
Norway.
Portugal with the
    Azores and Madeira.
Santo Domingo.
Servia.
Spain.
Sweden.
Switzerland.
Tunis.

United States of America.

A person who has filed an application for a patent for any invention in a Convention country other than Great Britain, prior to his British application, can obtain for his British patent the date of his application in this other country. Speaking generally, the date of the first application in any Convention country can be obtained for all subsequent applications for the same invention filed in other Convention countries up to the twelve-month limit.

In certain British possessions and foreign countries it is competent to file an application for a patent after the invention has been published; but generally for the more important countries the application must be filed before any publication takes place unless priority is obtained under the terms of the International Convention.

Every invention is not, of course, worth patenting abroad, even if the inventor has money to devote to this purpose; but in many cases it is advisable to apply for patents in a greater or less number of colonial or foreign countries. There are many important things to consider when debating the question of foreign patents and when to apply for these.

German Gebrauchsmuster.

In a case where a patent cannot be obtained in Germany for a modification in design which, although important and useful, would not be considered by the German Patent Office as suitable subject-matter for a patent, protection can be obtained by means of a "Gebrauchsmuster," which is not so valuable as a patent but which costs less. In some cases it is advisable to lodge applications at the same time both for a patent and a Gebrauchsmuster and only rely on the latter if the former is refused.

Delaying of Acceptance or Sealing of British Patent.

In the case of certain British possessions and certain foreign countries the period during which an application for a patent can be filed terminates a certain time after the date of sealing of the British patent for the same invention, and in the case of other countries the publication of the British specification prior to the application for a patent in these countries is a bar to the grant of a patent. It is, therefore, in many cases advisable to delay the publication of the British specification or the sealing of the British patent. In the normal course of events, the complete specification—and the provisional if there is one—are open for the first time to public inspection whenever the complete specification is accepted, i.e. passed by the examiner as satisfactory; and, in the absence of opposition,* the patent is sealed after the opposition period has elapsed and the sealing fee has been paid   Acceptance and sealing may however be delayed, if desired by the applicant, for a certain period without payment of a fee and thereafter to the maximum limit by payment of a fee or fees.   It is frequently expedient to effect delay, but each case must be considered on its merits.

Patents for Supplementary Inventions.

When an invention is supplementary to that for which a previous patent has been applied for or granted—if it is, for example, an improvement in, or modification of, the device or apparatus forming the subject-matter of the prior patent—the applicant may apply for a " patent of addition " instead of for an ordinary patent. The advantage of a patent of addition lies in the fact that the renewal fees which keep in force the " parent " patent also serve to maintain the patent of addition   A patent of addition has the disadvantage—often of little consequence—that it expires with the parent patent instead of running for fourteen years.

It rests with the Patent Office examiner to decide what constitutes good subject-matter for a patent of addition.

---

* For remarks on Opposition see page 27.

If it is decided that the invention is not what is considered to be good subject-matter for a patent of addition, and if this constitutes the only objection, it will be allowable to amend the application and apply for an ordinary patent, no loss of date or loss of stamp fees being incurred.

An application for a patent of addition, if made before the grant of the parent patent, must be made by the applicant or applicants for the latter, and, if made after the grant of the parent patent, must be made by the registered proprietor or the person for the time being entitled to the benefit of the parent patent. In cases other than Convention cases * any interested person may be joined as co-applicant.

There is no limit to the number of patents of addition which can be dependent on the one parent patent; but a patent of addition cannot be dependent on another patent of addition

Exploiting an Invention.

When an inventor is not in a position to directly make money from his invention by putting it into practice himself, it is of course necessary to come to an arrangement

* The " Convention " is discussed on page 36.

with a manufacturer   It is usually of advantage to the inventor to approach the manufacturer directly if this is possible; but sometimes another party can more readily secure an interview with the manufacturer or is in a position to negotiate better terms   In this connection it may be well to advise the inventor not to pay fees, except on the basis of commission, to any individual or firm who offers to arrange terms with manufacturers but is known to him only through advertisement or circular.   In that case, if no real service is rendered, no expense is incurred.

In submitting an invention to manufacturers or other parties with a view to exploitation, it is desirable to have a sample or model, if such will help the explanation; and the article exhibited should be as nearly as possible the exact likeness of what will be adopted in practice.   A bad model lowers the apparent value of the invention in spite of explanation as to how it can be improved.

It is not sufficient for the inventor to point out that his invention is on more scientific lines than what it is intended to replace, or even to show that it will be better for the user; it is important to show the manufacturer what he will gain by taking up the invention. The manufacturer naturally does not want to go to expense unless he can recover his outlay, and, moreover, he wants some substantial gain to compensate him for the risk and trouble that he is put to.

It may often be well for a patentee to agree to accept less remuneration than he considers himself entitled to. Many inventors are inclined grossly to overvalue their inventions, while others have too little business knowledge to estimate correctly the amount of royalty an invention will stand; others again are inclined to overlook the fact that it is natural for a licensee to require that there shall be a fair expectancy of making profits somewhat above the usual in ordinary competitive business, in order to compensate for the risk and trouble that are involved in taking up the invention.

Infringement.

An action for infringement of a patent cannot be commenced until the patent has been sealed; but damages may be obtained for infringement which has occurred before the date of sealing but after the date of acceptance of the complete specification.* Infringement may be by manufacture, use, or sale. Innocence is no defence to an action for infringement, but may be used as a defence to damages †

---

* Acceptance of complete specification is explained on page 27 under the heading " Opposition to Patent "

† See also " Marking of Goods," page 45.

The defender, whether denying or admitting infringement, can plead invalidity of the patent. If one claim of a patent is infringed, the Letters Patent is infringed; if one claim is invalid, the Letters Patent is invalid (But see remarks under heading "Amendment of Specification," page 46.)

The application for a patent for an invention which, if worked, would be an infringement of a patent of earlier date held by another party is no infringement of that patent, and is an act neither illegal nor unusual.

Neither a licensee nor a mortgagee can sue infringers.

Service of a writ in Scotland for infringement in England is competent.

Groundless Threats of Legal Proceedings.

A manufacturer or trader might suffer much loss through groundless threats of legal proceedings for infringement of a patent. The law provides that, if any person claiming to be the patentee of an invention, by circulars, advertisements, or otherwise, threatens any other person with any legal proceedings or liability in respect of any alleged infringement of the patent, any person aggrieved thereby may bring an action against

him, and may obtain an interdict against the continuance
of such threats, and may recover such damage (if any)
as he has sustained thereby, if the alleged infringement
to which the threats related was not in fact an infringement of any legal rights of the person making such
threats, provided that the latter individual does not with
due diligence commence and prosecute an action for
infringement of his patent.

Marking the Goods.

Innocence of the existence of a patent does not avoid
liability to damages for infringement as regards patents
granted before the end of 1907; but, as regards patents
granted thereafter, the defender may escape payment of
damages by proving that, at the date of the infringement,
he was not aware, nor had reasonable means of making
himself aware, of the existence of the patent. To avoid
this defence, patentees should see that goods according
to their patents are marked " patent " or " patented "
along with the number and year of the patent. The
word " patent " or " patented " without the number and
year of the patent will not suffice.

It is permissible to mark an article " patent " or
" patented " with or without the number and year of the
prospective patent, after the complete specification has

been accepted but before the patent is sealed. (An action for infringement cannot, however, be commenced until the patent is sealed.)

During the period between the filing of an application for a patent (either with a provisional or with a complete specification) and the acceptance of the complete specification, articles may be—and in general preferably are—marked " Provisionally Protected " or " Patent applied for."

Use of the Royal Arms.

The grant of Letters Patent does not confer on the patentee the right to use the Royal Arms

Amendment of Specification.

Reference has already been made to the amendment of a specification to avoid citations by the examiner (page 24). The applicant may, however, desire to amend his specification after acceptance and before grant of the patent, or the patentee may desire to effect amendment any time during the life of the patent. Facts may come to the knowledge of the applicant or patentee which convince him that his patent or prospective patent is invalid, or that the validity is doubtful, or that the specification contains an error or is not sufficiently clear

In such a case the applicant or patentee may apply for leave to amend. The application to amend must be made on a prescribed form. The Comptroller on receiving the application advertises the proposed amendment, and any interested party is given the opportunity of opposing it. The Comptroller—after hearing the opponent and the applicant in the case of opposition—decides whether, and under what conditions, if any, the amendment shall be allowed. The decision of the Comptroller is subject to appeal to the Law Officer (the Attorney-General or Solicitor-General for England).

No amendment is allowable which would make the specification, as amended, claim an invention substantially larger than, or substantially different from, the invention claimed before amendment.

Amendment as above mentioned is not competent when an infringement or revocation action on the patent in question is pending; but the court may by order allow the patentee to amend his specification by way of disclaimer.

Damages for " infringement " which occurred prior to an amendment which renders an invalid patent valid may in some cases be obtained if the patentee can prove that his specification and claims were originally framed in good faith and with reasonable skill and knowledge.

Assignation of Patents. *

A patent can be assigned only after grant, i.e., after sealing; but a patentee may, before grant, enter into an agreement to take all necessary steps (not already taken) to obtain a patent and thereafter to assign it. The latter procedure is common, and an agreement of this nature is enforceable. Assignation may be made to one or more individuals or to a body corporate.

An assignation of a patent may be either absolute or only in security, e.g., by way of mortgage. Except in the latter case the assignor parts with his whole interest, or part of his interest, as the case may be, and the action is final and irrevocable.† An assignation is made by a deed which is usually drawn up by the solicitor of the assignor or assignee.

There are many points to be watched when drafting or approving a draft of a deed of assignation, and it is thought that the following notes and suggestions will be of use.

---

* Throughout the book the familiar Scots term *assignation* is used in preference to the English term *assignment*.

† Absolute assignations have been chiefly in the author's mind when preparing these notes and suggestions, which may nevertheless be usefully considered in the case of a deed of assignation in security.

Consideration :

This may be a cash payment on execution of the assignation; it may consist of shares in a company, or of cash plus shares; or it may be a royalty depending on the number of articles sold and the size or schedule price of these, or depending on the net price actually obtained.

If the consideration is a royalty on sales, then it is in the interests of the assignor to have an agreement as to a minimum royalty per annum; otherwise the assignee might find it to be in his interest not to work the patent. The assignee might, for example, have a rival invention of his own which he could work without payment of any royalty, and it might therefore be in his interest to let the patent of which he was the assignee lie dormant. In the absence of a clause as to minimum royalty, or some other agreement of a like effect, the assignor would be powerless to obtain any remuneration or recompense.

Sometimes it is desirable to fix the price, or limits of price, of the patented article or articles.

Validity of Patent :

The assignor may guarantee the validity of the patent This is not, however, usual; but it is common for him to state that he has not done or omitted to do any act or thing which would render the patent liable to revocation.

D

[Assignations]

Future Improvements:

There may be a clause as to communication of future improvements and assignation of patent rights for these. This may be very necessary in some cases, because it frequently happens that an invention covered by a patent has not been fully tried when the patent is assigned, and the assignees may be dependent for commercial success on obtaining knowledge of, and the patent rights for, certain improvements necessary for satisfactorily working the invention If a clause relating to improvements and the like is included in the deed of assignation (or in a separate agreement), care should be taken to set forth, as clearly as possible, what is intended There may be improvements on the original invention, or there may be independent inventions which are quite different from the original but have the same object in view. The assignor may or may not be paid something additional for communicated improvements, but it is usually in the interests of the assignees to arrange that he shall benefit by these improvements. In the assignor's interest it should be laid down that the patent costs for these improvements be paid by the assignees; and in the assignees' interests it may be well to set forth (although this is perhaps not necessary) that the assignor will do all that is essential or desirable to allow of patents being obtained for the improvements.

Instructions and Working Drawings:

There may be a clause wherein the assignor undertakes to instruct the assignee or his servants as regards manufacture. The expense of this is sometimes borne by the assignor, but more often by the assignee. It may also be stipulated that drawings and other particulars will be given by the assignor to the assignee before a given date or when called upon. In the assignee's interests care should be taken in framing this clause.

Books and Inspection of Books:

When the remuneration is by royalty, there should be a clause wherein the assignee undertakes to keep books and permit inspection of these by the assignor or his representative.

Accounts and Payments:

Moreover, when the remuneration is by royalty, there should be a clause requiring the assignee to submit a written statement of account to the assignor at stated times, and to make payment of royalties at stated times.

Admission to Factory:

It may in some cases be to the advantage of the assignor to have a clause which gives him or his representative power to enter the factory of the assignee either with or without notice being given.

[Assignations]

Revocation or Declared Invalidity of Patent:

It will be in the interests of the assignee to have a clause whereby royalties shall cease if the patent should be revoked or declared in a Law Court to be invalid. This is of special importance when a minimum annual royalty is fixed.

Pushing the Sale:

It may sometimes be in the interests of the assignor to have a clause wherein the assignee undertakes to push the sale of the patented article and to supply the public to the extent of the demand. This is of importance if the consideration is a royalty on sales and if no annual minimum has been fixed.

Limited or Unlimited Assignation:

An assignation may be made for any limited and specified geographical area or may be unlimited. Any limitation should of course be set forth clearly in the deed of assignation, and it should be made clear whether the assignee has the exclusive right both to manufacture and to sell within his territory and whether he is prohibited both from manufacturing and from selling outside his territory.

When the assignation is unlimited geographically the assignee has all the rights previously held by the assignor;

when the assignation is limited, the rights of the assignee are of course necessarily restricted

Reservation of Right to Use the Invention:

If, in the case of a limited assignation, the assignor wishes to reserve to himself the right to use the invention in the assignee's area, this should be stated.

Maintaining Patent in Force:

Neither the assignor nor the assignee is under the obligation of maintaining the patent in force by paying the renewal fees unless there is a contract to this effect; moreover, in the absence of an undertaking, expressed or implied, the assignee is under no obligation to avoid risk of revocation or compulsory licence by working the patent in this country and supplying the reasonable requirements of the public.

Amendment or Surrender:

When for any reason the assignor is liable to suffer by the annulment or restriction of the patent, it will be in his interests to have a clause inserted wherein the assignee agrees not to surrender or amend the patent without the consent of the assignor. It is true that as an interested party the assignor would always have the option of opposing the action of the assignee, but he might neglect or be unable to do so

[Assignations]

Re-assignation, Further Assignations, and Licences :

It may in some cases be in the interests of the assignor to have a clause wherein the assignee undertakes not to re-assign or to grant licences without the consent of the assignor. Moreover, if the assignation is limited, it may be in the interests of the assignee to have some statement in the deed of assignation as to further assignations by the assignor

Export and Import :

The question of export to British Colonies or to foreign countries where there may be patents should not be overlooked; and care must be taken that, as regards the importation of goods made abroad under foreign patents, the assignor in the deed of assignation does not confer a right which he has already conferred on his foreign assignees or licensees.

Infringement :

When the consideration is by royalty, it will be in the interests of the assignor to have a clause wherein the assignee undertakes to sue infringers and to defend and use his best efforts to maintain the existence and validity of the patent for the full term.

Extension of Term of Patent :

There should as a rule be a clause providing for the possibility of an extension of term of the patent and providing that, if an extension of term is applied for and granted, the original patentee will obtain some substantial additional payment. The insertion of such a condition will not only be to the advantage of the original patentee, but will also be to the advantage of the assignee because there will be little chance of an extension of term being obtained unless the court is convinced that such extension of term will benefit the original patentee. (See page 34.)

Where the original patentee is the assignor, and the consideration is a royalty, it may not be necessary to have a special clause relating to extension of term; it may be sufficient in the clause or clauses relating to royalty to make it clear that royalties shall be paid during the whole life of the patent, including any extension of term.

Disputes and Differences:
It is well to have a clause providing for the settling of disputes and differences of opinion as to the interpretation of the deed of assignation, or as to occurrences which may not have been provided for.

Registration:
An assignation must be registered before the rights of the assignee are recognised at law.*

---

* See remarks on Registration on page 74.

Licences.

When an absolute assignation of a patent is made, the patentee, as already mentioned, parts with his whole interest, or part of his interest, as the case may be, and the action is final and irrevocable. On the other hand, when a patentee grants a licence to use the invention, he merely confers a right to the licensee to do that which he (the licensee) could not otherwise do without infringing the patent. The licensor still remains owner of the patent The licensee cannot, for example, bring an action for infringement, or seek leave to amend the specification, or offer to surrender the patent, without the consent of, and the use of the name of, the licensor. If a patentee dies after having granted a licence and during the term of the licence, his rights pass to his legal representatives, and any royalties which would have been due to him are then payable to his heirs.

A licence may be " exclusive " or " general " An exclusive licence confers on the licensee the sole right to manufacture, use, or sell; and the licensor obliges himself not to grant licences to any other person during the term of the licence. The licensor may in such a case reserve to himself the right to manufacture. If he does not expressly reserve this right, he can be restrained by the licensee. If an exclusive licence is granted for the whole term of the patent and if the licensee has power to grant sub-licences, then he possesses nearly all the rights which were previously held by the patentee. He cannot, however, as aforesaid, bring an action for infringement, or petition for amendment of the patent, but he may pay all the expenses in connection with an action for infringement, or other action, and thus sue in the name of the licensor, with his consent. Exclusive licences are quite common. In fact, in many cases a firm will only accept a licence on the condition that it is exclusive. If a licence is exclusive, the licensee can fix his own selling price as he will have no competition. He may therefore be able to pay heavy royalty. If the licence is not exclusive, however, he knows that he will run the risk of competition by other licensees.

A general licence as opposed to an exclusive licence leaves the licensor power to grant other licences in respect of the same patent. Licences of this nature also are common. In many cases it would not be possible for one firm to obtain all the possible orders in connection with an invention, and the licensor will receive better remuneration by granting several licences rather than one exclusive licence.

The question as to whether it is better for a patentee to grant an exclusive licence or not is often a difficult one.

[Licences]

If the invention is a pioneer one and if there is, and is likely to be, nothing else on the market which can compete with the article or substance covered by the patent, it may be better for the licensor to endeavour to get some firm to pay a high rate of royalty for an exclusive licence.

An exclusive licence, with a high rate of royalty, granted to a single firm might result in the licensor obtaining more remuneration than he could hope to obtain from royalties from a large number of firms, because, in the absence of competition, all purchasers would have to approach the sole licensees, who would, therefore, be able to sell practically the same amount as would be represented by the aggregate sales of a number of licensees. Moreover, the sole licensees, being in possession of a monopoly, would be able to obtain a higher price for the patented article than would be the case if several firms were licensed and were in competition.

In many cases, however, it would not be to the advantage of a patentee to grant an exclusive licence, and in other cases the patentee may find it impossible to arrange satisfactory terms with a single manufacturing firm.

Licences are divided above into two classes—exclusive and general; they can also be divided in another way —namely, into those which are limited geographically and those which are without geographical limitation. A licence can be granted for the whole of the country covered by the patent, that is to say, in the case of a British patent, for the United Kingdom and the Isle of Man, or alternatively it may be granted for only a particular portion of the United Kingdom (or the Isle of Man). The one licence is sometimes called a limited licence and the other an unlimited licence, but these terms are sometimes used to express other meanings.

Licences can be divided in still another way, namely, voluntary licences and compulsory licences A voluntary licence is one which is granted voluntarily by the patentee, or a licence granted under the terms of an agreement which has been voluntarily drawn up between the parties. A compulsory licence is one that is granted by order of the Board of Trade or the Court. Particulars regarding the granting of compulsory licences will be given later.*

A licence may be granted by deed, but not necessarily so. In fact there is no requirement by law as to the particular manner in which a licence may be granted; a licence given by a verbal agreement has been, and may be, held to be quite valid. Moreover, an agreement

---

* See page 69.

to grant a licence for a fixed term is equivalent to granting a licence, that is to say, it can be enforced.

A mere licence in writing to use the invention, if not
by deed and not in the nature of an agreement, requires
no stamp; but a licence is usually in the form of a deed
or agreement, when a stamp is necessary, the value of
the stamp depending upon the circumstances.

A mere licence without a contract can be revoked at
will, but such licences are seldom granted. A licence
is usually coupled with a contract, and a term is also
fixed. The term may be for the whole life of the patent.
or for any number of years. It may, moreover, be laid
down that the licence can be determined by either party
on giving a certain prescribed notice.

A licensee cannot question the validity of the patent
unless the licensor has expressly warranted validity. It
is not usual for the licensor to do this. The licensee can,
however, refer to the state of public knowledge at the
date of the patent for the purpose of showing the scope of
the claims, that is, he may seek to show that the claims
should be construed in such a manner that they do not
cover what he is manufacturing, and therefore no royalty
is due from him. There is, however, nothing to prevent
an ex-licensee from raising the question of the validity of
the patent in an infringement action.

In a contract in relation to a licence, conditions which would restrict the licensee with regard to the use of the article made according to the patent, or as regards the purchase of accessories, may, as set forth in the Patents and Designs Act, 1907, be ineffectual as being in restraint of trade and contrary to public policy. The law on this point is somewhat unsatisfactory; and, in the author's opinion, there are very few conditions which cannot be inserted in a licence contract if both parties are agreeable to these conditions and if the conditions are set forth in a suitable manner.

It will be obvious from what has been said that the drawing up of a licence indenture or agreement calls for considerable skill and attention Unless certain things are clearly expressed and certain eventualities provided for, disputes are likely to occur; and either party, unless his interests are properly guarded, may find himself in a position very different from what he expected.

It is thought that the following notes and suggestions may be of use in drafting or approving a draft of a licence agreement.

Term of Licence:
The term of the licence should of course be stated. The term may extend to the date of expiry of the patent;

to some earlier date; or until determined. In the last case it should of course be made clear how and when the licence can be determined. If the term of the licence extends to the date of expiry of the patent, a statement should be made as to whether or not, in the event of extension of term of the patent being obtained, the licence is automatically continued during this extended term.

Consideration or Royalty:

It is usual for the licensor to receive remuneration in the form of a royalty. The royalty may be reckoned on the number of articles sold and their size or scheduled price, or it may depend on the net price actually obtained. It is usually in the interests of the licensor to stipulate that a minimum annual royalty be paid. This is specially important in the case of an exclusive licence. (See remarks on minimum royalty on page 49.)

Sometimes a sum of money is paid on the signing of the licence agreement, and this may either constitute part of the royalties paid in advance or may be in addition to the royalties.

In the case of a general licence (that is, a non-exclusive licence) it will be in the interests of the licensee, especially if the licence cannot be determined for several years, that the licensor should bind himself not to grant better licence terms to other licensees

It may sometimes be necessary for the licensor to fix the selling price, or to place a limit on the selling price, of the articles on which royalty is to be paid. This is usually not so necessary when a minimum royalty is fixed.

Infringement:

The licensee should require the licensor to undertake to commence without delay proceedings against infringers, or to allow his name to be used by the licensee for such proceedings. In the latter case he will himself take action. It should be made clear as to whether the licensor or the licensee undertakes to bear the expense of infringement actions. Sometimes it is stated in the licence indenture that, if the licensor fails to take proceedings against infringers, the licensee can determine the licence. This in most cases will not, however, be good enough for the licensee.

Sub-Licences:

It is submitted that the licensee has no power to grant sub-licences unless this power is expressly given to him, but it is usual in the licence indenture to make a definite statement one way or the other. In some cases the licensee is given power to grant sub-licences only to parties approved by the licensor.

[Licences]

A licensee is responsible to the licensor for royalties for manufacture by a sub-licensee unless there is a contract to the contrary.

Mortgage :

It is common for the licensee to undertake not to mortgage his licence without the consent of the licensor.

Scope of Licence:

It should be made clear that the licence is for manufacture, use, and sale, or if not, then for what. This is specially important in the case of a licence limited geographically. A licensee might, for example, have liberty to manufacture his goods in any part of the United Kingdom, but be restricted as regards the sale of the goods to a particular portion of the country Again, he might be at liberty to manufacture anywhere within the United Kingdom; be allowed to sell anywhere within the United Kingdom; and be permitted to export to certain specified countries abroad. Many other arrangements are feasible. The question of importation of goods made abroad according to the invention should be rendered quite clear, and in some cases of general (non-exclusive) British licences it may be necessary for the licensee to require the licensor to undertake, in granting licences to foreign firms, to prohibit these foreign firms from sending goods into the United Kingdom.

If in the case of an exclusive licence, the licensor wishes to reserve to himself the right to manufacture or to use or to sell within the area covered by the licence, this will require to be stated.

Renewal Fees:

It is desirable that a statement be made as to whether renewal fees are to be paid by the licensor or the licensee. It is usually the licensor who undertakes to do this. If the licensor is to pay the renewal fees, then it is in the interests of the licensee that the licensor should undertake to have each payment effected a certain period before the last usual day for payment, so that when this day arrives the licensee can assure himself that the payment has been effected.

Defending a Revocation Action:

It is in the interests of the licensee to have a clause wherein the licensor agrees to defend a revocation action either at his own expense or at the expense of the licensee.

Working the Invention:

As a patent may be revoked on the ground that the invention has not been worked to meet the reasonable requirements of the public, or has been worked wholly or mainly abroad, it may be in the interests of the

E

licensor to require the licensee to undertake to work the invention to an adequate extent within the United Kingdom.

Marking of Goods:

It may be in the interests of the licensor to require that the licensee shall mark every article made according to the invention (or the wrapper or the like in which it is contained) with the number and year of the patent. (For reasons for this see page 45.)

Moreover, if the licensor wishes to familiarise the public with a name which he has given to the article made according to the invention, he may require all articles to be stamped with and invoiced under this name. This question of a name may be of very great importance to the licensor in a case where the licence is, or may be, of short duration. If the name is a registered trade mark, then, after the termination of the licence, the late licensee will not be able to use this name, but a new licensee will have the right to do so with the consent of the licensor.

Books and Inspection of Books:

See this sub-heading under " Assignation of Patents," page 51.

Accounts and Payments:

See this sub-heading under "Assignation of Patents," page 51.

Admission to Factory:

See this sub-heading under "Assignation of Patents," page 51.

Instructions and Working Drawings:

See this sub-heading under "Assignation of Patents," page 51.

Future Improvements:

See this sub-heading under "Assignation of Patents," page 50.

Pushing the Sale:

See this sub-heading under "Assignation of Patents," page 52.

Bankruptcy or Liquidation of the Licensee:

It may be well in the licensor's interests to have a clause to the effect that the licence is terminated *ipso facto* if the licensee becomes bankrupt or insolvent, or, being a limited liability company, goes into liquidation.

Amendments or Surrender:

There should be a clause relating to amending the specification. It is submitted that this clause might well be to the effect that, if either party considers that the specification should be amended, then the parties should meet and try to come to terms, and, if they fail to come to terms, the matter should be submitted to arbitration. Or the clause might be to the effect that the licensor shall not apply to the Comptroller for leave to amend the specification without the approval of the licensee. (This latter alternative will not always be good enough for the licensee.)

It may be of advantage to the licensee to require the licensor to agree not to offer to surrender the patent without the consent of the licensee.

Revocation or Surrender or Declared Invalidity:

If the licensee is due to pay a minimum annual royalty, it will probably be in his interests to have a clause whereby this shall cease if and whenever the patent shall cease to be in force or be declared in a law court to be invalid. This may not be necessary in the case of surrender, but, in the case of declared invalidity, and even in the case of revocation against the will of the patentee, it would appear that, in the absence of an agreement to the contrary, the licensee is liable for any stipulated royalty until the licence agreement is determined.

The law allows a licence agreement to be determined by either party any time after the patent—or, if more than one, all the patents—has ceased to be in force, by giving three months' notice to the other party, notwithstanding anything in the agreement to the contrary.

Assignation of Patent:

It may in some cases be advisable to provide for the assignation of the patent, as the licensee's interests might be affected through a transfer of the patent rights making him liable to account to another party.

Disputes and Differences:

As in the case of assignations it is well to have a clause providing for the settling of disputes and differences of opinion as to the interpretation of the licence agreement or as to occurrences which may not have been provided for

Compulsory Licences.

What has already been said in the preceding section on licences has been intended to refer specially to voluntary licences   It is necessary to discuss shortly compulsory licences   Any interested party may present a petition to the Board of Trade alleging that the reasonable requirements of the public with respect to any patented invention have not been satisfied, and praying for the grant of a compulsory licence or for the revocation of the patent.

[Licences]

The presentation of such a petition may cause the parties to come to terms, and a voluntary licence may result. In the absence of an agreement the Board of Trade, if satisfied that a *primâ facie* case has been made out, refers the petition to the Court—in the case of Scotland to a Lord Ordinary of the Court of Session. If, on the other hand, the Board of Trade is not satisfied that a *primâ facie* case has been made out, it dismisses the petition.

When such a petition is referred by the Board of Trade to the Court, the patentee is heard as well as the petitioner; and any person claiming an interest in the patent, as exclusive licensee or otherwise, is also heard. The Law Officer—or such other counsel as he may appoint—is also entitled to appear and be heard.

When it is proved to the satisfaction of the Court that the reasonable requirements of the public with reference to the invention have not been satisfied, the patentee may be ordered by the Court to grant licences on such terms as the Court may think just. If the Court is of opinion that the reasonable requirements of the public will not be satisfied by the granting of licences, it may order the revocation of the patent. The Court cannot, however, order the revocation of a patent before the expiration of three years from the date of the patent; neither can it order the revocation at any date if the patentee gives satisfactory reasons for his default.

An order by the Court directing the granting of a compulsory licence operates as if it were embodied in a deed granting a licence.

As regards what is meant by the reasonable requirements of the public, the Patents and Designs Act, 1907, states that :—

" the reasonable requirements of the public shall not " be deemed to have been satisfied—

" (a) if, by reason of the default of the patentee " to manufacture to an adequate extent and supply " on reasonable terms the patented article, or any " parts thereof which are necessary for its efficient " working, or to carry on the patented process to an " adequate extent, or to grant licences on reasonable " terms, any existing trade or industry, or the estab- " lishment of any new trade or industry, in the " United Kingdom is unfairly prejudiced, or the " demand for the patented article, or the article " produced by the patented process, is not reason- " ably met; or

" (b) if any trade or industry in the United King- " dom is unfairly prejudiced by the conditions " attached by the patentee, before or after the pass- " ing of this Act, to the purchase, hire, or use of the " patented article or to the using or working of the " patented process."

Revocation of Patent.

The subject of revocation of a patent is somewhat complex. A patent may be revoked .—

(a) by order of the Court on direct petition to the Court;

(b) by order of the Court on reference to the Court by the Board of Trade following a petition to the Board of Trade;

(c) by order of the Comptroller on application to him.

To discuss the subject-matter fully would be a too lengthy matter for this book, but the chief facts are as follows :—

The Court may, on direct petition to the Court, order the revocation of a patent on the ground that it was obtained in fraud of the rights of the petitioner, or that the invention had been manufactured, used, or sold, within the United Kingdom by the petitioner before the date of the patent. Proceedings for revocation in the Scottish Courts take the form of an Action of Reduction.

The Court may order the revocation of a patent as an alternative to the grant of a compulsory licence on reference to the Court by the Board of Trade following a petition to the Board of Trade. (See remarks under heading "Compulsory Licences," page 69.)

The Comptroller may order the revocation of a patent on the application of any person who would have been entitled to oppose the grant of the patent on any one of the grounds on which the grant of the patent might have been opposed.*

The Comptroller may order the revocation of a patent on the application of an interested party on the ground that the patented article or process is manufactured or carried on exclusively or mainly outside the United Kingdom. An application on this ground cannot, however, be made less than four years after the date of the patent. When such an application is made the Comptroller first considers whether or not the allegations are correct If he decides that they are incorrect he dismisses the application; but if he decides that they are correct, it does not necessarily follow that he will order the revocation of the patent. The patentee is given an opportunity of proving, if he can, that, even although the manufacture in this country has been small or nil, there were good reasons for this. If the Comptroller is not satisfied with

---

* The grounds on which a patent may be opposed are given on page 27 et seq.

F

the patentee's representations, he may either make an order revoking the patent forthwith, or he may allow the patentee a definite period in which to manufacture to an adequate extent within the United Kingdom. Moreover, the period allowed by the Comptroller may afterwards be extended.

The Comptroller may order the revocation of a patent on the application of the patentee. This is referred to under the heading of "Surrender of Patent" on page 35.*

Registration of Deeds, Etc.

A register is kept at the Patent Office wherein are entered the names and addresses of patentees and notifications of assignations, licences, amendments, extensions, revocations, &c.   Assignations, licences, mortgages and the like ought as a rule to be recorded in this book   Forms of application for registration are prescribed and must be stamped : the stamp fee is usually ten shillings.

---

* For further discussion of the subject " Revocation of Patent " the reader is referred to the " Patents and Designs Act, 1907," Sections 24, 25, 26 and 27, and to larger works on Patent Law and Procedure.

Patent Office Publications.

The Patent Office issues printed copies of specifications of patents about three weeks after acceptance. These printed specifications can be purchased at the Patent Office or obtained by post on receipt of an order on a prescribed stamped form, or an order without a remittance if the purchaser has a deposit account at the Patent Office.

The Patent Office issues a weekly journal in which particulars are given of applications filed, complete specifications filed and accepted, patents sealed, renewal fees paid, &c. This journal also contains abridgments of the specifications of patents—but not in any case until after the complete specification has been accepted.

The abridgments of patents specifications are also published by the Patent Office in classified book form, about 1300 non-overlapping complete volumes having already been issued. Another 271 volumes are at present in preparation, and there are in addition about 100 old volumes of abridgments which are to a slight extent overlapped.

The Patent Office also publishes quarterly and yearly name indexes of applications for patents, quarterly subject-matter indexes of applications, and monthly, quarterly, and yearly subject-matter indexes of complete specifications accepted.

Working Inventions in Secret.

The question often arises as to whether it is better to work an invention in secret or to apply for a patent or patents. The question is largely a commercial one and cannot be adequately dealt with in this volume. It may be pointed out, however, that if A invents, decides not to apply for a patent and proceeds to work in secret; and B thereafter invents independently what is substantially the same, B is entitled to a patent, and A cannot prevent his obtaining one. The cases in which it is preferable to work in secret rather than to apply for a patent comprise, in the author's opinion, only a small minority.

Sometimes an inventor attempts to obtain a patent and still keep his invention, or an essential part of it, a secret. He should be warned against attempting this dangerous and really fraudulent procedure. A patent is granted as recompense to an inventor for disclosing his invention to the public and showing how it can be worked to advantage; and insufficient disclosure of the invention is sufficient ground for upsetting a patent.

INDEX

—

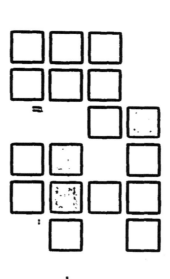

Lightning Source UK Ltd.
Milton Keynes UK
UKHW020756260522
403565UK00006B/380